9781800654617

AF126799

THE mythical creatures TAROT GUIDEBOOK

THE
mythical creatures
TAROT GUIDEBOOK

Jayne Wallace
Illustrations by Julia Cellini

CICO BOOKS

For Tracey

Your honesty, openness, and fierce trust in yourself have shown me the power of doing the same. This deck is rooted in that spirit—truth, trust, and seeing clearly.

Thank you always.

Published in 2025 by CICO Books
An imprint of Ryland Peters & Small Ltd
20–21 Jockey's Fields   1452 Davis Bugg Road
London WC1R 4BW   Warrenton, NC 27589
www.rylandpeters.com
Email: euregulations@rylandpeters.com

10 9 8 7 6 5 4 3 2 1

Text © Jayne Wallace 2025
Illustration © Julia Cellini 2025
Design © CICO Books 2025

The author's moral rights have been asserted. All rights reserved. No part of this publication may be reproduced, stored in a retrieval system, or transmitted in any form or by any means, electronic, mechanical, photocopying, or otherwise, without the prior permission of the publisher.

A CIP record for this book is available from the British Library.
US Library of Congress CIP data has been applied for.

ISBN: 978 1 80065 461 7

Printed in China

Editor: Caroline West
Desk editor: Imogen Valler-Miles
Senior designer: Emily Breen
Art director: Sally Powell
Creative director: Leslie Harrington
Head of production: Patricia Harrington
Publishing manager: Carmel Edmonds

The authorized representative in the EEA is
Authorised Rep Compliance Ltd.,
Ground Floor. 71 Lower Baggot Street,
Dublin, D01 P593, Ireland
www.arccompliance.com

Safety note: The safe and proper use of candles and incense is the sole responsibility of the person using them. Do not leave a burning candle unattended. Never burn a candle on or near anything that might catch fire. Keep candles out of the reach of children and pets.

MIX
Paper | Supporting responsible forestry
FSC® C106563

contents

Introduction 6
Reading the Cards 8
How to Approach a Reading 10
The Spreads 12

The Major Arcana 16

0 The Fool 18
I The Magician 20
II The High Priestess 22
III The Empress 24
IV The Emperor 26
V The Hierophant 28
VI The Lovers 30
VII The Chariot 32
VIII Justice 34
IX The Hermit 36
X The Wheel of Fortune 38
XI Strength 40
XII The Hanged Man 42
XIII Death 44
XIV Temperance 46
XV The Devil 48
XVI The Tower 50
XVII The Star 52

XVIII The Moon 54
XIX The Sun 56
XX Judgment 58
XXI The World 60

The Minor Arcana 62

The Suit of Swords 64
The Suit of Cups 92
The Suit of Wands 120
The Suit of Pentacles 148

Acknowledgments 176

introduction

This deck has been a dream of mine—a special addition to my tarot collection that feels truly personal.

Since childhood, I've felt deeply connected to the magical creatures in my dreams, especially dragons. I feel as if they've always been my spirit guides—a symbol of strength, wisdom, and protection. As many of you know, I am fascinated by the ocean, too. I am drawn to all the underwater mysteries of Atlantis and the merfolk who live there. Scuba diving deepened this connection for me, giving me a feeling of stepping into another world, one that inspires me both spiritually and creatively.

In this deck, the Major Arcana are brought to life by mythical creatures, each one carefully chosen to reflect the deep magic held within the cards. I see those creatures as guardians of wisdom, transformation, and fate. Each suit within the Minor Arcana is celebrated by a different mythical being, which is linked to its own elemental energy: Swords and dragons (Air), Cups and merfolk (Water), Wands and phoenixes (Fire), and Pentacles and dryads (Earth).

For as long as I can remember, Tarot has been my strongest link to the spirit world. It's more than a tool; it's part of who I am. But for a long time, I kept that side of me hidden. Like so many of us with a deep intuition or spiritual gift, I tried to push it aside. I realized, though, that Tarot was my calling. It has always guided me, given me clarity, and helped me to connect with others on a profound level. I'm still learning all the time, too, whether through spirit, my everyday experiences, or the incredible people I meet through Tarot.

Tarot isn't just about guidance; it opens doors, reveals possibilities, and helps us to see our life's journey with greater clarity and purpose. When shuffling my deck, I feel the presence of my spirit guides and guardian angels. Taking a few deep breaths, I open myself up and the messages come through clearly. It's an incredible feeling—one I'm now honored to share with others.

My love for Tarot has even inspired me to create my own wellness products, each one made with intention and guided by spirit. Every candle, mist, and crystal is handpicked and infused with the same energy I put into my readings.

Tarot isn't just about predicting the future; it's about understanding yourself and your journey, while noticing the signs all around you.

I can't wait for you to experience the magic of this deck for yourself.

Jayne Wallace

reading the cards

The 78 cards in the deck fall into two groups: 22 Major Arcana cards and 56 Minor Arcana cards. The Major Arcana (see page 16) reveals major turning points, while the Minor Arcana (see page 62) expresses day-to-day events. As with playing cards, the minors fall into four suits: Cups, Pentacles, Swords, and Wands. I have chosen a mythical creature to represent each suit—on the Cups cards are merfolk, with dryads (also known as tree nymphs) on the Pentacles, dragons on the Swords, and phoenixes on the Wands.

In this book, you will find details about each card as well as its interpretation and meaning. Each card features a principal keyword for instant connection, and there are additional keywords to provide deeper or alternative associations. Also included is a Mythical Message for each card, which represents the guidance being sent to you, offering you insight into how to understand your situation better. There is also an affirmation for each of the cards. The affirmations are there to assist you in rituals that allow you to move forward and bring positive change to your life.

As you become more confident reading cards for yourself and others, you may find that you don't need to look up the meanings of the cards but naturally connect with the images, which are specially designed to appeal to your intuition.

MESSAGES FROM MYTHICAL CREATURES

Mythical beings have captured the imaginations of people around the world for thousands of years. They have been a source of inspiration for ancient legends and folklore through the ages and continue to captivate us in contemporary literature, movies, and television. Deeply symbolic, they can provide us with valuable insights to help us make sense of ourselves, our lives, and the world around us.

MYTHICAL CREATURES IN THIS DECK

Centaur: With the upper body of a human and the lower body of a horse, centaurs appear in Greek mythology and can be associated with wisdom and courage.

Cerberus: A ferocious three-headed dog from Greek mythology, Cerberus guarded the entrance to the Underworld. Its three heads could represent conflicting directions.

Dragon: From destructive fire-breathers to wise and powerful protectors, the portrayal of dragons varies widely across numerous cultures, as does their symbolism and meaning.

Dryad: In Greek mythology, dryads are nymphs, or spirits, of trees, woodlands, and forests, embodying the beauty of nature.

Fairy: Appearing in the folklore of many cultures, "fairy" is often used broadly to describe a mythical human-like creature. Fairies are frequently depicted with wings.

Faun: Half-human and half-goat, fauns appear in Roman mythology and are often portrayed as a man with the legs, tail, horns, and ears of a goat. They can represent the forces of nature.

Griffin: With a lion's body and the head and wings of an eagle, a griffin symbolizes strength, protection, and bravery.

Hippogriff: With an eagle for the front half and a horse for the hind half, the hippogriff is a beacon of power and balance.

Kraken: In Norse folklore, krakens were enormous, squid-like sea monsters, capable of crushing entire ships with their powerful tentacles, representing destructive forces.

Merfolk: Also called mermaids and mermen, merfolk have the upper body of a human but the tail of a fish, and they dwell in the world's oceans.

Naiad: In Greek mythology, a naiad is a water nymph who lives in flowing water such as rivers and streams. They can embody the nurturing qualities of water.

Pegasus: Usually depicted as a graceful, winged white horse in Greek mythology, Pegasus symbolizes freedom.

Phoenix: With links to several cultures, a phoenix is a mythical bird with fiery plumage, capable of rising from its own ashes to be reborn; an emblem of transformation and renewal.

how to approach a reading

Before you begin, honor the ritual of tarot reading by finding a quiet room with a table and comfortable chair. You may like to light some incense or a candle to create a sacred space, extinguishing these when your reading is over.

1 Set your intention: Focus on giving yourself, or the person you are reading for, the best possible reading that is available to you with your cards.

2 Choose a spread: Decide which card layout you are going to use before you shuffle and select your cards, so you'll know in advance how many cards you will need to lay down. Choose any spread from this book that you feel drawn to (see pages 12–15). If you are reading for another person, choose a spread for them.

3 If you are reading for yourself: Shuffle the deck, thinking about what you would like to know, as if you're shuffling your question into the cards. Do this for a minute or two. If you cannot think of a question to ask, just keep an open mind. Place the shuffled deck face down, making a fan shape. Feel your hand being drawn to certain cards, then select them and place them face down in the spread arrangement you have chosen.

4 If you are reading for someone else: Ask that person to shuffle the cards. During this process, they should keep an open mind and ask a question, aloud or silently. While this is happening, take a few deep breaths and focus on the process. Ask the person to place the deck face down, split it into two piles, and place the bottom pile on top. Take back the deck and deal the cards from the top, placing them face down in the spread arrangement you have chosen.

5 Turn the cards and begin: Turn the cards face up and let your intuition guide you to a meaning based on the image on the cards and/or refer to the interpretations on pages 18–175. If a card is upside down, just turn it the right way up. I don't include meanings for reversed (upside-down) cards in this deck, as they are often negative.

6 Finishing your reading: When you have finished the reading, say thank you with your inner voice for the guidance you have received, as you give the cards a final shuffle to cleanse and reenergize them. Gather up the cards, wrap them in silk or another fabric to protect them, then place them in a box or drawer until you are ready to read again. Extinguish the incense or candle.

TIP

When reading for another person, the only time they touch the cards is at the beginning of the reading, when shuffling, dividing, and reassembling the deck ready for you to lay out in a spread. At the end of the consultation, if that person has a specific question they would like answered, ask them to say it out loud. Then take the top card on the deck and lay it down to give the answer.

the spreads

ONE-CARD Q&A SPREAD

This is a simple, yet powerful spread that offers instant clarity when you need some quick guidance. Whether you're seeking an answer to a specific question or a general message from the Universe, a single card can provide deep insight. Focus on your question while shuffling and when you feel ready, draw the top card. This is your message. Trust your intuition and the wisdom the card reveals.

PHOENIX RISE: THREE-CARD SPREAD

Symbolizing transformation and rebirth, the Phoenix Rise spread helps you to understand where you've been, where you are, and where you're headed. This is a great three-card spread for understanding patterns in your life, and how past actions influence your present. If you're feeling stuck, this spread can reveal what needs to be released and where new opportunities are emerging. Shuffle with intention, then draw three cards to reveal your journey through time and lay them out as shown.

1 PAST

2 PRESENT

3 FUTURE

Tip: After reading the first three cards, you can draw another set of three cards and layer them over the first for extra insight. This will offer more context or show potential challenges ahead. You can also draw a third layer, if you wish.

MANIFEST YOUR DREAMS: FOUR-CARD SPREAD

Like water flowing toward its destination, this spread guides you in aligning your dreams with action. It illuminates what you desire, how your career and finances play a role, as well as the steps you need to take to achieve success, and the potential outcome. This is an excellent spread for those working toward a goal or who want to understand what's blocking their progress, encouraging clarity and taking inspired action. Shuffle the deck while visualizing your dream life, then draw four cards and lay them out as shown.

1 Wishes: What do you truly desire? This is your guiding star.

2 Career/Money: How does your professional or financial path align with your dreams?

3 Achievements: What steps will help you reach your goal?

4 Outcome: What is the potential outcome of your current path?

1

4

2

3

THE SPREADS

WEEKLY SPREAD: SEVEN CARDS FOR THE WEEK AHEAD

Ground yourself and find balance with this structured weekly reading. Each card represents a day of the week, offering insight into the opportunities and challenges ahead. By looking at the week to come, you can align your actions with your intentions, creating a sense of clarity and purpose. Draw seven cards, one for each day, starting with Sunday, and lay them out as shown.

1   2   3   4   5   6   7

1 Sunday: Overall energy for the week ahead.
2 Monday: The focus for the start of the week.
3 Tuesday: Challenges or opportunities arising.
4 Wednesday: Midweek shifts or new perspectives.
5 Thursday: Momentum building or obstacles appearing.
6 Friday: What to reflect on or release.
7 Saturday: How to recharge and prepare for the next cycle.

DRAGON'S LAIR: EIGHT-CARD ARCH SPREAD

This spread helps you navigate the unseen—secrets, hidden truths, and the power of your mind. It's ideal for times of confusion, helping you to unravel the complexities and reveal the truths behind a situation. If you are feeling mentally overwhelmed, then Dragon's Lair brings clarity and direction. Select eight cards and lay them out as shown.

1 Secrets/Hidden Truths: What's beneath the surface?

2 Understanding Situations: What must you acknowledge or accept?

3 Accomplishing Goals: How can you move forward with intention?

4 Movement: Where is your energy best directed?

5 Challenges/Obstacles: What is blocking you?

6 Vision: What bigger perspective should you consider?

7 Contemplation: What requires deeper thought or patience?

8 Answer: The final message or resolution.

Tip: Think of this spread as venturing through a dragon's lair, with each card revealing a new layer of insight. Start by uncovering hidden truths, then work your way through the challenges before reaching the final card, which holds the key to clarity and action.

THE MAJOR ARCANA

The 22 cards of the Major Arcana highlight important decision points and events in your life and are considered to be the core and foundation of the deck.

The Major Arcana cards represent various aspects of the human experience. They take us on a journey—the hero's journey, from the beginning (0 The Fool) right through to the completion of a phase and fulfillment (XXI The World). Like life, all experience is there: the joys and the sorrows, the victories, the defeats, and the redemptions.

Each card embodies a powerful archetype or lesson that can help clarify your intentions and help you to make informed decisions and foster a deeper understanding of yourself and the world around you. You can use the cards as tools for reflection, decision-making, and guiding your path toward your desired outcomes. By working with the Major Arcana, you align yourself with the energies and stories they represent. At first, you can practice your readings using just the Major Arcana cards, as a way to get to know the cards, before moving on to read with the full deck.

0 THE fool
faith

trust, protection, freedom, naivety

At the edge of a cliff stands The Fool, gazing out over cloud-covered mountain peaks. Before him, a great dragon is weaving through the mist, its golden scales shimmering like beacons of possibility. Will he make the leap? Behind him, a small, silver-white dragon watches, a guardian of intuition, whispering quiet reassurance. There's an innocence in The Fool's stance, but also anticipation. This is the first step into the unknown, where adventure and risk live side by side. The journey begins, and the only way is forward.

MEANING It is time to take a leap of faith, as life is pushing you toward the edge of the mountain. Trust in what you want and look at what inspires you through the journey of the Tarot. The Fool reminds you that stepping into the unknown is necessary for growth, so embrace it with excitement rather than fear. This card represents new beginnings, boundless potential, and the freedom to explore without hesitation. Having faith is the key to your journey, as the Universe is protecting and guiding you. Move forward with courage, curiosity, and an open heart.

MYTHICAL MESSAGE Have faith in all that you do.

AFFIRMATION
my journey is just beginning

I THE **magician**
reassurance

power, action, connection, movement

The Magician stands with one hand reaching to the sky and the other pointing to the earth, a bridge between vision and reality. Behind him, a powerful dragon spreads its wings, exhaling soft smoke in the shape of an infinity symbol. Endless potential surrounds him. In front of him, a glowing crystal altar holds the four sacred tools—sword, cup, pentacle, and wand—waiting to be used. The Magician is the master of his own fate, turning ideas into action, dreams into something real. With focus and skill, he shows that anything is possible.

MEANING You may feel that you are juggling many things in your life right now, but The Magician assures you that you have everything you need to succeed. This card brings power, action, and the ability to manifest your desires through focus and intention. Never doubt yourself! Life is calling for you to be strong and determined. When you align your mind, heart, and spirit, you can create the reality that you seek. Stay confident, trust in your abilities, and take inspired action. The Universe is responding to your energy, so use it wisely.

MYTHICAL MESSAGE Although you may feel that everything is up in the air at present, build on your knowledge and look for change.

AFFIRMATION
I have everything I need within me

II THE high priestess
guidance

*spirituality, psychic abilities,
learning, meditation*

A graceful naiad, The High Priestess floats in an underwater world of deep blues and shimmering light. Tiny, glowing fairies dance around her. One carries an ancient book, its pages filled with hidden wisdom, waiting to reveal itself in the right moment. The High Priestess is calm and still, yet her energy is powerful. She doesn't search for answers; she understands that truth comes in its own time. Wrapped in the quiet magic of the unknown, she reminds us to trust our intuition and listen to the whispers beneath the surface.

MEANING It's time to find unity within all your spiritual knowledge, working closely with your spirit guides and guardian angels. The High Priestess asks you to listen to your intuition and trust the wisdom within, becoming more open, aware, and empathetic to your environment. She is the keeper of hidden truths, guiding you to look beyond the surface and into the deeper meaning of life. Meditation, reflection, and spiritual learning will bring you closer to understanding your path.
Be patient: The answers will come with divine timing.
Trust the mysteries that unfold and embrace the power of your inner knowing.

MYTHICAL MESSAGE Understanding your own spirituality is the key to increasing your intuition.

AFFIRMATION
I trust my intuition and inner wisdom

III THE empress
femininity

nurture, inner beauty, motherliness, abundance

The Empress is surrounded by Mother Nature's lush greenery with a great bear watching over her; not a threat, but a quiet guardian and symbol of the protective power of nature. Dressed in flowing greens, she holds a staff in one hand, while her crown is adorned with delicate flowers, a symbol of creation, love, and abundance. Everything around her is growing, thriving, and full of life. There is a sense of warmth and safety, like stepping into a place that truly cares for you. She represents fertility in all forms: new ideas, new beginnings, new life. The Empress is a reminder that when we nurture what we love, it thrives.

MEANING Feel the motherly energy and love radiating from The Empress. She is a symbol of nurture, abundance, and creation, guiding you through times of self-doubt and helping you to embrace your inner beauty. The Empress reminds you to take care of yourself, honor your emotions, and trust in the natural cycles of life. You could be about to create something new—a project, or a relationship, or to work on personal growth. Know that what you pay close attention to will flourish. This card invites you to connect with nature, embrace love in all its forms, and recognize the power of softness and strength within you.

MYTHICAL MESSAGE Be open to your own femininity because it is time to find your inner self.

AFFIRMATION
abundance flows freely to me

IV THE emperor
stability

structure, leadership, mentoring, empowerment

The Emperor, a regal faun-like figure crowned with antler-like branches, stands tall in the forest clearing. He blends natural power with a quiet authority, holding both a staff and your gaze, while a phoenix rises in a blaze of golden fire behind him. The flames spill into the earthy woodland, revealing both movement and stillness: The Emperor is a ruler in terms of law and order but also of transformation held within a firm structure.

MEANING The Emperor brings strength and stability to your life. His presence offers guidance when you need discipline, leadership, and clear direction. Call upon him when you are seeking a strong, fatherly influence, one that provides both love and honest wisdom. Creating a solid foundation will bring long-term success and it's time for you to stand tall and trust in your ability to lead. The Emperor encourages you to take control where needed, set clear boundaries, and make decisions with confidence. Stability and order will help you move forward with purpose.

MYTHICAL MESSAGE Find your inner masculinity to give you confidence for clear communication.

AFFIRMATION
I stand strong in my power

V THE hierophant
inner wisdom

intention, values, spirituality, authority

A centaur draped in flowing robes, The Hierophant stands with a large pentacle glinting in his raised hands and casting light over two figures who kneel in recognition before him. Around his neck hangs a single key, a symbol of access to inner wisdom and knowledge. The air feels still, as though the moment itself is part of an ancient ritual, filled with gentle authority and a shared knowledge that invites you subtly inward.

MEANING Be guided by your inner light, as The Hierophant encourages learning, tradition, and spiritual growth. This card speaks of seeking knowledge, whether that's with a teacher or mentor, or through your own deep reflection. Reminding you that wisdom is found in both structure and intuition, The Hierophant calls on you to align with your values and beliefs, ensuring they support your true self. If you are searching for answers, trust that the right guidance will come. Embrace spiritual teachings, rituals, or practices that resonate with you because they will lead you forward on your path. Trust in the lessons that are unfolding.

MYTHICAL MESSAGE New pathways and challenges are opening up, so feel the positive energy around you.

AFFIRMATION

I embrace wisdom and guidance

VI THE lovers
decisions

passion, emotions, detachment, love

The Lovers move together, yet remain separate. The female, glowing in shades of blue and purple, gazes off into the distance, lost in her own thoughts. The male, bright in reds and golds, looks at her with deep devotion. They exist in harmony, drawn to each other but never lost within one another. Their dance is one of dilemma, between love and independence, connection and choice.

MEANING You may feel deeply connected within your relationships, yet something still feels unsettled or distant. The Lovers remind you that love is not just about passion, but also about choice and alignment. You may need to make decisions regarding your long-term commitments, whether romantic or personal. This card wants you to seek honesty, balance, and mutual understanding. If you feel torn, listen to your heart. What is truly in alignment with your soul's path—love or self-discovery? The Lovers invite you to move with intention, ensuring your choices are based on truth rather than illusion.

MYTHICAL MESSAGE Open your heart to love, affection, and inner happiness.

AFFIRMATION

I love and accept myself fully

VII THE chariot
purpose

hastiness, speed, success, motivation

Two winged horses surge forward: One light, full of clarity and inspiration; the other dark, embodying strength and resilience. Together, they move with purpose, perfectly in sync and guided with precision, their momentum unstoppable. The contrast between the horses isn't conflict; it's balance. Their opposing forces drive The Chariot forward, proving that success comes not from strength alone, but from harmony between strength and having a clear vision.

MEANING The Chariot signals movement, success, and motivation, yet you may be feeling as if you are being pulled in two opposing directions. Rather than making hasty decisions, take a moment to find balance and clarity in what you truly need. This card represents determination and willpower, urging you to take charge and steer your life with purpose. Challenges may arise, but with focus and inner strength, you will overcome them. Trust in your ability to navigate obstacles and keep your eyes on the bigger picture. Stay disciplined, remain confident, and move forward with a clear vision; success is within your reach.

MYTHICAL MESSAGE Moving hastily is not always the right pathway to success. Removing the struggle sets you free.

AFFIRMATION
I am in control of my own destiny

VIII justice
victory

balance, legalities, honor, fight

Justice rides a powerful hippogriff, suspended between night and day. The crescent moon rises as the sun sets behind her, casting a perfect balance of light and shadow. In one hand, she holds a sword, sharp and unwavering. In the other, her golden scales are delicately balanced. Her gaze is steady, her crown a symbol of wisdom and divine judgment. There is no deception here; only truth, seen and measured. The hippogriff's wings beat against the sky, carrying her forward with certainty. Every action has consequences, and Justice ensures they are met with fairness and clarity.

MEANING Justice calls for you to stand in your truth and fight for what is rightfully yours. This card represents fairness, balance, and the consequences of your actions. If you are facing an important decision, weigh up your options carefully, ensuring that honesty and integrity guide you toward the answer. Justice is a reminder that everything finds its balance in time, and what you put out into the world will return to you. If you have felt wronged, know that fairness will prevail. Stand firm, trust the process, and believe that truth and honor will always lead to victory.

MYTHICAL MESSAGE The fights of life are coming to end, and you can almost feel the victory.

AFFIRMATION
I make choices with clarity and fairness

IX THE hermit
withdrawal

solitude, overwhelmed, calmness, seclusion

In the low light in front of a stone castle, The Hermit moves through the shadows, carrying a lantern filled with fireflies, their golden glow spilling out to illuminate his path. In his other hand, a weathered staff steadies his steps. The air is thick with solitude and reflection, as he embraces the silence of the night, the dim surroundings mirroring his inward journey. His path is not about where he walks but what he discovers within himself.

MEANING Life may feel overwhelming right now, but The Hermit invites you to step back and seek solitude. This is not about isolation, but finding clarity in stillness. When the world feels heavy, turning inward will bring the answers you seek, so take time to reflect, meditate, or withdraw from outside distractions. The Hermit shows you that wisdom comes in quiet moments, and by taking some space to feel those moments, you will reconnect with your inner light. Whether seeking guidance or simply a pause, allow yourself the time to find peace, because the answers you need are already within you.

MYTHICAL MESSAGE Spend time with the people who matter the most to you, even if you are feeling overwhelmed and in need of time for yourself.

AFFIRMATION
I find wisdom in solitude

X THE wheel OF fortune
manifestation

recognition, movement, change, luck

A vibrant dragon coils gracefully around a glowing Zodiac wheel filled with the rhythm and energy of each sign. As the dragon spirals through the air, there is a clear sense of motion, change, and momentum. There is no beginning nor end here, only the endless turning of life's cycles. It is here that coincidences unfold, with fortune favoring those who move with change, not against it.

MEANING The Wheel of Fortune turns in your favor, bringing change, movement, and divine synchronicity. This is a card of destiny; what is meant for you is aligning effortlessly. Trust in the cycles of life; every shift, whether expected or sudden, is guiding you toward something greater. Luck and opportunity are at your fingertips, but your mindset determines how you receive them. Stay open to unexpected blessings because fortune favors those who embrace change. Everything is happening just as it should, bringing expansion and abundance your way.

MYTHICAL MESSAGE What you believe, you create; spin the wheel with intention.

AFFIRMATION
I welcome change and new opportunities

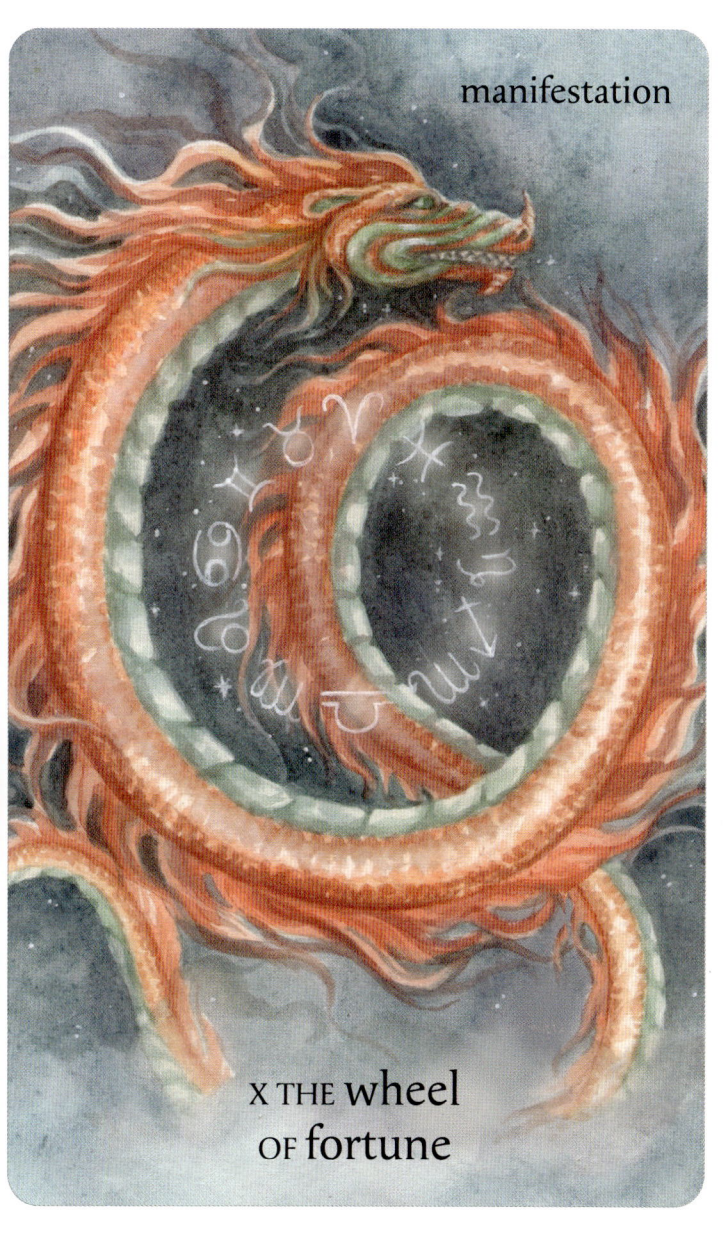

XI strength
domination

persuasion, control, understanding, knowing

A woman with fiery red hair cradles the face of a majestic griffin. As she holds its head gently, their eyes meet and, in that gaze, there is no fear, only trust. The griffin's golden feathers shimmer in the light, powerful yet calm. Strength is not about force but understanding, not about control but respect. Together, they embody the quiet power of courage and compassion.

MEANING Strength is not just about your physical being but also your inner resilience, patience, and understanding. True power comes from balance; taming any storm within, without losing your kindness. You may be facing challenges that require control and composure, but know that you have the ability to navigate them with grace. You could also be dealing with difficult people or internal struggles, but trust that your calm, steady presence is your greatest asset. Strength reassures you that you are more capable than you realize and you do not need to force outcomes. Quiet confidence will always guide you through.

MYTHICAL MESSAGE Find the strength to open your mind to being in control of what your heart desires, because this is the time to feel your inner power.

AFFIRMATION
I am courageous, resilient, and strong

XII THE hanged man
stagnation

transformation, change, sacrifice, integrity

A serene merman, The Hanged Man dangles upside down, his shimmering tail caught in the tangles of an old fishing net. Coral surrounds him and anglerfish cast a soft, eerie glow, forming a halo around his peaceful face. Although trapped, he does not resist. He is not afraid, but surrenders to the stillness, understanding that sometimes the only way forward is to let go. In the silence of the ocean, a new perspective begins to form.

MEANING The Hanged Man offers a moment of pause, inviting you to surrender and trust in divine timing. Right now, you may feel suspended between where you are and where you want to be. But rather than seeing this as stagnation, consider it a sacred time of transformation. This card asks you to shift your perspective. What if this waiting period is a gift, offering you clarity before your next step? Embrace the stillness, for it holds deep wisdom. The answers will come when you stop forcing them.

MYTHICAL MESSAGE A pause in life helps you see what you really want.

AFFIRMATION
I surrender and trust the process

XIII death
transition

letting go, rebirth, empowerment, change

From the earth's core, a kraken-like creature appears, its tentacles winding through the wreckage of a sunken ship. Yet alongside fish swimming in the wreck, there is a small section of coral starting to grow, the subtle signs of life beginning to bloom from what's been broken. Daylight faintly filters from the ocean surface, and although the scene speaks of destruction, it also holds a beauty, the kind that can exist only when something has been let go.

MEANING Death brings a positive transformation, urging you to release what no longer serves you. This is not an end, but a powerful rebirth. You must let go of something in your life—a belief, habit, or situation—to make space for these new beginnings. Although change can often feel unsettling, the Death card assures you that it is for your greatest good. Embrace the cycle of endings and rebirths, with the knowledge that what comes next will align more closely with your true path. Trust in the process and allow yourself to step into the new chapter that awaits you.

MYTHICAL MESSAGE Embrace life's changes because there will always be a positive outcome.

AFFIRMATION

I release the old and embrace transformation

XIV temperance
calmness

healing, relaxation, hope, wellness

At the base of a waterfall stands an angel in bare feet, with wings glistening in the fine mist. One foot dips into the flowing water, the other is grounded on rock, creating a quiet balance between emotion and earth. One hand holds a glowing red fairy, its soft light filled with healing energy. Behind the angel, a phoenix rises in soft white with hints of fiery red, a nod to new beginnings rooted in the tranquility. The air feels still, as if the world is pausing, with everything existing in gentle harmony and each element flowing effortlessly into the next.

MEANING Temperance wants you to find balance and healing in your life. This is a time to take control of your energy, giving yourself the space to recharge and realign. If life is feeling chaotic, step back and reconnect with a sense of inner calm. Temperance teaches patience: Things are unfolding exactly as they should, bringing hope, even if progress feels slow. Trust that harmony will come as you move forward with grace. Allow your guides and intuition to bring messages of peace and reassurance. Through balance and moderation, everything will fall into place.

MYTHICAL MESSAGE Open your heart to close friends and family and allow their healing and love into your life.

AFFIRMATION
I am balanced in mind, body, and spirit

XV THE devil
boundaries

addiction, hardship, honesty, freedom

Hidden deep within a volcanic cave, Cerberus snarls and strains against loose chains. The heat is intense, raising tensions further. Each of the three heads pulls in a different direction, the eyes glowing with fire and frustration. The chains that bind Cerberus look breakable, but they stay put. Although caught in a place of friction and desire, freedom is there for the taking, simply waiting to be claimed.

MEANING The Devil appears when you are feeling trapped, restrained, or caught in unhealthy cycles. This card signals addiction; not just in the physical, but also in emotional and mental attachments that are no longer serving you. It is time to reassess your boundaries and reclaim your freedom. Are you giving away your power? The Devil is a reminder that you always have a choice. By acknowledging what holds you back, you can begin to break free. Release any self-imposed limitations, step into your truth, and move forward with confidence.

MYTHICAL MESSAGE Remember that the thing that binds you is loose. You can step out from it and find your freedom.

AFFIRMATION
I break free from what no longer serves me

XVI THE tower
upheaval

destruction, entrapment, foundations, chaos

A tall, stone tower stands high above the jagged hills, its walls blackening and cracking in the flames. Two dragons have The Tower in their grip. They unleash streams of furious flames that consume the spire. Sparks fly into the smoke-filled sky as parts of the structure start to collapse. Tiny figures rush to escape through shattered windows. But, at the base, the foundation holds strong, untouched by the chaos above. Destruction is everywhere, but beneath it all something endures.

MEANING The Tower shakes the foundation of your life, bringing sudden change, upheaval, and revelations. While it may feel chaotic, trust that this is a necessary shift. Something in your life was not built to last, and now you have the opportunity to rebuild with clarity and strength. Resistance will only prolong discomfort, so allow the old structures to fall. From this, new wisdom emerges, and you gain the power to create something even stronger. This is not an ending but a powerful transformation. What's rebuilt from the rubble will be unshakable.

MYTHICAL MESSAGE A steady foundation is essential for rebuilding and improving any situation.

AFFIRMATION
I rise stronger from life's challenges

XVII THE star
wishes

intention, positivity, serenity, optimism

Beneath a deep blue sky, a woman kneels at the edge of a river, pouring water with quiet intention. She gazes into the water, lost in the reflection. Above her, a great dragon floats in midair, wings stretched wide and holding a radiant star between its claws. All around them, the constellations are scattered like crystals and a crescent moon watches in stillness. There is gentle, whispered magic here, with space to breathe, to soften, to wish, and to heal.

MEANING The Star is your guiding light after the darkness, bringing inspiration and optimism. This card invites you to make a wish and trust that better days lie ahead. Your dreams are valid, and the Universe is ready to support them, so now is the time to set clear intentions. Healing is taking place, even if it is not immediately visible. Let go of any fear and align yourself with the energy of possibility. The Star reminds you that your light is powerful, and your desires are within reach if you believe in them fully.

MYTHICAL MESSAGE Focus on what your heart desires because your dreams will come true.

AFFIRMATION
I believe in my dreams and my future

XVIII THE moon
illusion

sadness, depression, contemplation, friendship

A full moon hangs in the night sky, its silvery light casting a rippling reflection on the ocean below. The water glows, blurring the line between reality and illusion, while at the shoreline, crayfish slowly emerge, just like inner truths gradually revealing themselves. Above the ocean, two ethereal dragons weave through the mist and around the moon. They move like a dream, offering guidance through uncertainty. This card is a soft, glowing invitation to trust what is felt, not just seen, and to embrace the unknown with intuition.

MEANING The Moon casts a veil of illusion, making things seem unclear or uncertain. You may feel lost in your emotions, unsure of what is real and fearing people's perceptions. This card encourages deep reflection. Are you seeing things as they truly are, or through the pain of past wounds? You may be keeping parts of yourself hidden, afraid of being vulnerable, but true strength lies in authenticity. Allow others to see the real you and don't be afraid to accept help when you need it. Clarity will come in time; trust that your inner wisdom will guide the way.

MYTHICAL MESSAGE Never feel alone because there is always someone to show you a good deed.

AFFIRMATION
I embrace both my light and my shadow

XIX THE sun
joyfulness

memories, happiness, lightheartedness, vitality

A beautiful phoenix soars across the golden sky, its fiery wings trailing wisps of orange and red through the air. Below, on a sunlit beach, two children laugh as they play in the warm sand, their joy as bright as the day itself. The world feels full of life and possibility. This is a moment of pure happiness, a reminder that light always returns, bringing with it warmth, renewal, and boundless energy.

MEANING The Sun is a card of pure joy, success, and vitality. It shines a light on your path. This is a time filled with happiness and abundance, as you step into a phase of confidence and fulfillment. Life feels bright, and your energy is renewed. It is time for you to enjoy the here and now, celebrating just how far you've come. Your inner light is magnetic, attracting all sorts of positivity toward you. Express gratitude and share your joy because everything is unfolding in your favor.

MYTHICAL MESSAGE Spread your joy to others to bring a little light into someone else's day.

AFFIRMATION
I shine with joy and confidence

xx judgment
self-blame

hardship, reflection, visions, evaluation

A phoenix rises from a bed of glowing ash, flames threading through its wide, feathered wings. The air pulses with motion in orange, red, and gold, blending into one powerful wave of transformation. At the center of the fire, the phoenix flickers between bird and something more celestial—part creature, part spirit—showing that this is not just rebirth, it is reckoning.

MEANING Judgment calls for deep self-reflection and release. You may have been carrying some guilt, regret, or self-blame, and have been allowing the past to weigh heavily on your heart. This card urges you to let go of these burdens; what has happened cannot be changed, but you have the power to move forward with clarity and self-compassion. Growth comes from learning, not from punishing yourself. It is now time to forgive, heal, and step into a new phase of your journey, free from the chains of past mistakes. Embrace this moment of awakening and trust in your personal evolution.

MYTHICAL MESSAGE Don't allow life to weigh you down. Let go of the guilt and free yourself of past pain.

AFFIRMATION
I step into my true purpose

XXI THE **world**
completion

achievement, movement, success, union

Two hands gently cradle a glowing earth. Circling around it, the four elements—Air, Water, Fire, and Earth—form a protective ring, represented by a sword, a cup, a wand, and a pentacle. These aren't just nods to the tarot suits; they are the anchors of something deeper, aligning harmony, balance, and movement. Everything is in its place and everything is connected; there is wholeness written in the stars.

MEANING The World brings you movement and change. You have reached the end of an important cycle and now is the time to celebrate your growth as you open up to new opportunities. Everything you've worked for is coming together, and you are stepping into a place of wholeness. This card reminds you that endings bring new beginnings; life is ever-evolving and you are ready for the next adventure. Embrace the lessons you've learned and carry them forward with confidence. You are aligned with your purpose and the Universe is supporting your journey.

MYTHICAL MESSAGE It is time to celebrate because you have completed your cycle.

AFFIRMATION
I celebrate my growth and success

THE MINOR ARCANA

The Minor Arcana cards reveal everyday events. The 56 cards are divided into four suits: Swords, Cups, Wands, and Pentacles.

Each suit contains 14 cards: ten numbered cards and four court cards—Page, Knight, Queen, and King. The four suits have an associated mythical creature, element, and energy. The elements are Air, Water, Fire, and Earth, which guide us toward the suit's energy or overall meaning.

Suit	Mythical Creature	Element	Energy
Swords	Dragons	Air	Represents intellect, conflict, and clarity through the power of the mind, and winds.
Cups	Merfolk	Water	Associated with emotions, intuition, and the depths of the soul, flowing like water.
Wands	Phoenixes	Fire	Embodies creativity, action, and the transformative forces of fire and passion.
Pentacles	Dryads	Earth	Represents stability, abundance, and the grounding nature of the earth.

The court cards can represent influences and symbolize people in our lives and individuals we come across. Pages might stand for youthful people, but also denote new phases and beginnings. The Knights can indicate figures in our lives who are vigorous and brave, and reflect periods of activity and action. The Queens embody wise, experienced figures in our lives and are indicators of power, potential, and advice. The Kings can signify authority and power, in the form of both people but also situations. They also point to drive and ambition.

ace of swords
cutting through

victory, triumph, truth, clarity

With wings wide open, the dragon lifts its sword high—clear, bold, and full of power. The dragon's gaze is filled with renewed strength and clarity. This is a fresh start and an important breakthrough moment.

MEANING A surge of clarity cuts through your confusion, revealing truth and direction. This card marks a powerful mental breakthrough where old doubts dissolve and a path forward becomes clear. Trust your intellect and act with confidence. You can overcome challenges when you focus on what's real and strip away distractions. The Ace of Swords reminds you that truth is powerful—use it wisely, and success will follow.

MYTHICAL MESSAGE Clarity strikes like lightning. A breakthrough is here, so trust in your truth and cut through any illusion in your way.

AFFIRMATION

clarity helps me cut through confusion

two OF swords
choices

preference, transition, indecision, logic

A dragon emerges from the forest's edge; two swords are laid out before it, each pointing toward a different pathway. The forest is quiet, as if holding its breath while a choice is being made. The way forward begins with a clear decision.

MEANING You're hesitating between two options, unsure which way to go. The longer you avoid the decision, the more stuck you feel. The Two of Swords asks you to trust your intuition—deep down you already know what aligns with your truth. This transition may be uncomfortable, but clarity will come only when you face the situation directly. Remove the blindfold and move forward.

MYTHICAL MESSAGE Avoiding a decision won't make it easier. Open your eyes, trust your instincts, and choose the path that feels right for you.

AFFIRMATION

uncertainty is only temporary

three OF swords
disheartened

betrayal, heartbreak, release, loss

In front of a storm-fueled sky, with an open chest and revealing a pierced heart, the dragon's pain is raw and honest. You can almost feel the ache, but there's something strong in that openness, as if the healing has already begun.

MEANING A painful truth has come to light, and it hurts. Whether this is heartbreak or betrayal, ignoring it won't make it go away. The Three of Swords encourages you to acknowledge your emotions rather than push them aside. Pain is temporary, but avoiding it only prolongs the time it takes to heal. Let yourself process what has happened, knowing that this experience, though difficult, will bring growth and clarity.

MYTHICAL MESSAGE Heartache is painful, but facing it leads to healing. Acknowledge your emotions—this storm will pass and clarity will follow.

AFFIRMATION
I allow myself to feel and to heal

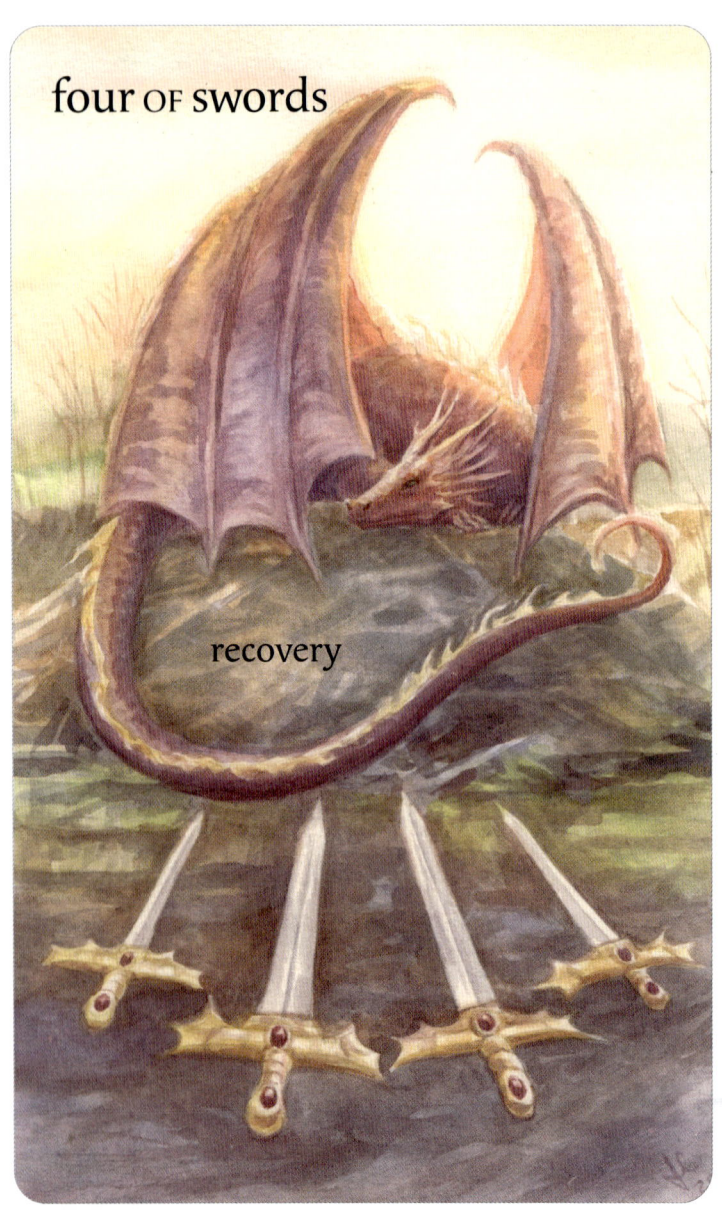

four OF swords
recovery

rest, isolation, stillness, relaxation

Curled up peacefully in the golden glow of the sun, the dragon's face is calm and at ease. The four swords point inward, surrounding, but not touching, its body. There is an air of protective energy. This is a space for recovery, reflection, and stepping away from the noise.

MEANING It's time to pause and recharge. The Four of Swords appears when you've been pushing too hard and need a moment of stillness. You've been dealing with exhaustion, stress, and conflict. This card is a reminder that stepping back isn't failure, but essential. A little self-care goes a long way, allowing you to return with fresh energy and a clearer perspective. Give yourself permission to take a break.

MYTHICAL MESSAGE Rest isn't weakness; it's necessary. Step back to clear your mind and regain strength for life's next phase.

AFFIRMATION
I give myself permission to rest

five OF swords
bereavement

stagnation, release, conflict, pettiness

A dragon stands on a cliff edge, breathing out fire shaped like a sword, with four other swords resting nearby. On lower ground there are small figures who are poised for battle but will soon retreat. There is a feeling of unease while the dragon stands tall—the victory feels complicated and unsettled.

MEANING A recent conflict may have left you feeling empty rather than victorious. The Five of Swords asks you to reflect. Was the conflict worth it, or did pride and ego take over? Sometimes winning comes at too high a cost. If you're caught in a cycle of tension, consider letting go. Releasing the need to be right and not dwelling on past battles will bring true peace.

MYTHICAL MESSAGE A hollow victory benefits no one. Let go of resentment and learn from the conflict. Choose growth over unnecessary battles.

AFFIRMATION

I choose peace over proving a point

six OF swords
inner peace

freedom, trust, progress, journey

Gliding low over a calm lake, the dragon skims the surface while following a small boat carrying six swords. There's a feeling of slow movement. This movement is not loud, but it is meaningful: it represents moving forward with care.

MEANING You're moving away from a difficult situation, even if the movement is not easy. The Six of Swords represents transition and healing, leaving behind what no longer serves you and trusting that better things lie ahead. Change can feel uncertain, but this shift is necessary. Allow yourself to let go and embrace the peace that's waiting. The past does not define your future.

MYTHICAL MESSAGE You're moving on from a difficult period. Trust the journey ahead—even if this feels uncertain, it leads to a calmer, more stable place.

AFFIRMATION
healing is a journey I honor

seven OF swords
clarity

betrayal, dishonesty, trickery, manipulation

Flying high across fields of gold, the dragon clutches three swords. Four have slipped from its grasp and are falling. The pace is fast and the moment tense. There is a sense of something being taken, or being held too tightly to carry well.

MEANING Something isn't adding up, and your instincts know it. The Seven of Swords warns of secrecy, whether from someone else or within yourself. Avoiding the truth won't help, and deception, even with good intentions, never really ends well. This is a time to be strategic but also honest. Pay attention to what's happening around you, and don't ignore red flags. Truth will come to light.

MYTHICAL MESSAGE Not everything is as it seems. Be mindful of deception, including your own. Seek the truth and act with integrity.

AFFIRMATION

I trust my instincts and protect my energy

eight OF swords
forgiveness

freedom, analysis, self-doubt, control

Head hung low and wings tied by rope, the dragon is surrounded by eight swords, a trap with no way out. The energy is heavy and closed in. But there's space beyond those blades, and maybe more than can be seen at first glance.

MEANING You feel trapped, but is this real or just fear holding you back? The Eight of Swords suggests that your limitations may be self-imposed. Doubt and overthinking have you feeling caged in, but the key to freedom lies in your hands. Shift your mindset, challenge negative thoughts, and release your past mistakes. Forgiving yourself allows you to break free and move forward with confidence.

MYTHICAL MESSAGE You're never trapped. Shift your perspective and break free from self-doubt, taking back your power.

AFFIRMATION
freedom starts with how I see myself

nine OF swords
healing

restlessness, doubt, stress, fear

Hunched beneath a moody sky, the dragon sits with eyes closed, heavy with worry. Above, nine swords float in a curve—sharp and glowing faintly in the darkness. The weight of the situation is obvious, but the glimmers in the sky show there is always a way forward.

MEANING Worry is keeping you awake, as you replay those worst-case scenarios in your mind. The Nine of Swords acknowledges your fears but reminds you that they are often bigger in your head than they are in reality. It's time to confront them instead of letting them control you. Seeking support and grounding yourself in the present will help to ease the weight of doubt and fear.

MYTHICAL MESSAGE Worry keeps you up at night, but the fear is not the reality. Face your anxieties and, when you have acknowledged them, they'll lose their power.

AFFIRMATION

I acknowledge my fears without letting them overwhelm me

ten OF swords
adjust

ending, acceptance, suffering, breaking point

The dragon lies still on a rocky riverbank, ten swords embedded in its back. Everything is still. Whatever happened is done. It's the end of something; a final, painful release before anything new can begin.

MEANING Something has reached breaking point, and while this ending may feel painful, it also brings a release. The Ten of Swords marks a difficult but necessary conclusion—one that is clearing the way for something new. Accepting what's over will allow you to move forward without the weight of the past. This is not just an ending; it's the first step toward renewal.

MYTHICAL MESSAGE Endings may feel painful, but they bring freedom. Release the past and trust that new beginnings lie ahead.

AFFIRMATION

endings create room for renewal

page OF swords
action

curiosity, knowledge, enthusiasm, new perspective

Sword held firmly with both hands, the Page stands alert and ready for action. A dragon circles above, watching and waiting for her next move. Unfazed by the dragon's presence, the Page is ready to take control of the situation.

MEANING A thirst for knowledge is driving you forward. The Page of Swords is eager to learn, asking questions and exploring new ideas. Now is the time to stay sharp and observe carefully, thinking ahead before making any moves. Be curious, but mindful; sometimes your enthusiasm can lead you to jump in too soon. Gather your information and trust your intelligence. It will put you in the best possible place for what's to come.

MYTHICAL MESSAGE Stay sharp and ask questions. New information is coming, so be open and ready to act when the time is right.

AFFIRMATION

I don't need all the answers to make a start

knight OF swords
success

ambition, impulsiveness, drive, action

The Knight leans forward, sword raised and cloak flying behind him as the dragon rises up in challenge. Everything about the Knight is fast, focused, and sure. His eyes are locked on the horizon; the path is chosen and the chase is on. He's not here to hesitate; the moment is now.

MEANING The Knight of Swords moves fast, charging ahead with determination and, sometimes, without thinking. Ambition is driving you and success is within your grasp, but being impulsive could create a setback. This card encourages you to take action, but with strategy rather than recklessness. Being bold is powerful when paired with foresight. Use your energy wisely and you'll make great progress without all the obstacles.

MYTHICAL MESSAGE Charge ahead with confidence, but don't rush without thought. Strategy will turn your ambitions into real and lasting success.

AFFIRMATION

I act with focus and drive

queen OF swords
intention

strong will, structure, directness, fairness

The Queen sits on her throne in the quiet after the storm, sword raised with purpose; not in threat, but in truth. In the distance, a dragon glides with silent authority—a symbol of the wisdom the Queen has earned. There's undeniable clarity in her stillness, the kind that comes from lived truth. She doesn't rush or soften. Her presence alone cuts through confusion, seeing exactly what needs to be seen.

MEANING The Queen of Swords sees things clearly and speaks with purpose. She values truth over illusion and makes decisions with intelligence, not emotion. Her strength of character urges you to adopt the same mindset, helping you to cut through confusion, set clear boundaries, and trust your ability to lead. Now is the time for structure and intention. Be strong, but don't lose sight of compassion.

MYTHICAL MESSAGE Cut through confusion with your wisdom and clarity. Speak the truth and set boundaries for your intelligence to lead the way.

AFFIRMATION
I speak with honesty and intention

king OF swords
honesty

integrity, ethics, rationality, logic

Crowned and composed, the King sits on his throne at the summit of a rocky mountain overlooking his kingdom, sword resting in his hand: not raised, but always present. His face hints at the calm knowing of someone who's seen through illusion. His steady gaze and relaxed posture show complete trust in his own mind. There's no need to ask for authority; it settles around him naturally.

MEANING The King of Swords leads with wisdom, logic, and fairness. His decisions are guided by integrity, favoring head over heart, which can come across as lacking in emotion. This card calls on you to step into a position of authority, letting people know where they stand with you. Whether in your career or home life, approaching a difficult conversation with clear thinking and honesty will serve you best. Stay true to your principles and success will come through careful, ethical decision-making.

MYTHICAL MESSAGE Lead with logic and fairness, staying true to your values. Trust that your knowledge is your greatest strength.

AFFIRMATION
I see clearly and make decisions wisely

ace OF cups
flowing emotions

love, abundance, new beginnings, intuition

A giant cup overflows from the waterfall above, spilling into the surrounding pool below where three beautiful mermaids are relaxing in the flowing water. There's a deep connection between them, the water, and the moment, one of emotional fullness that asks for nothing more. Their hearts overflow with abundance.

MEANING A new emotional chapter is beginning and the Ace of Cups brings an overflow of love and deep connections. This could be a new love, a self-discovery journey, or new doors opening. This card invites you to open your heart fully and make space for the abundance that is coming. Allow your emotions to flow freely. What's starting now has the potential to bring true fulfillment.

MYTHICAL MESSAGE Something stirred a spark of deep emotion or a new beginning for you. Let it flow naturally and trust where it leads.

AFFIRMATION

I open my heart to love and connections

two of cups
partnership

entwinement, love, mutual respect, union

A touching meeting in an underwater world, two merfolk offer their cups to each other, mirroring one another with grace. There's something tender in this moment, balanced and intentional. It is a mutual offering where a connection begins, not with words but with reciprocal understanding.

MEANING A deep bond is forming. The Two of Cups brings a synergy and mutual respect to your relationships; romantic, platonic, or professional, this connection is built on a genuine understanding of, and trust in, each other. Unity creates strength, so nurture this partnership, communicate openly, and allow it to grow and flourish. This has the potential to develop into something truly meaningful.

MYTHICAL MESSAGE Genuine connections are rare. When you find one, cherish it. Relationships built on trust and balance have the power to grow into something long-lasting.

AFFIRMATION

I give and receive love in equal measure

three OF cups
unity

collaboration, enjoyment, community, friendship

Three merfolk raise their cups in celebration, forming a loose circle that's part of a shared rhythm with the current. There's unity here in this small, joyful gathering that feels easy and true. There is strength in their togetherness.

MEANING Celebrating connection and a shared joy, the Three of Cups shines light on the happiness around your friendships, supporting one another, and belonging to a community. It's a time for coming together, appreciating those around you, and enjoying the good times. Shake off stress and have a laugh with those closest to you, because life's best moments are meant to be shared.

MYTHICAL MESSAGE This is a time for togetherness. Surround yourself with those who uplift you and relish the joy that comes from shared celebrations.

AFFIRMATION
I celebrate with those who lift me higher

four OF cups
meditation

reevaluation, apathy, contemplation, disappointment

A merman sits alone on a rock, head bowed, lost in thought. Three cups nearby are untouched, while a fourth rises from the water's surface, offered by a patient hand. Nothing is being demanded, but what is being offered will be noticed only if he changes his gaze.

MEANING Feeling disconnected or uninspired? The Four of Cups suggests introspection but warns against missing out on opportunities. If boredom or discontentment are clouding your perspective, shift your focus. Sometimes, what you need is right in front of you, so stay open to new possibilities and don't let stagnation hold you back.

MYTHICAL MESSAGE When nothing feels quite right, take a step back. Don't let boredom or disappointment shut you off from unexpected opportunities.

AFFIRMATION

stillness brings clarity and new insights

five OF cups
mourning

loneliness, depression, regret, sorrow

A merman stands waist-deep in water, still in the midst of the movement around him. Three cups lie on their side on the shore, their contents spilled and lost. Behind the figure, two cups remain upright, waiting. Strands of seaweed drift around his body, caught between motion and stillness, as if something is loosening gently and beginning to let go.

MEANING Loss and disappointment weigh heavily, but not all is gone. The Five of Cups acknowledges your grief but reminds you to look at what remains. Healing begins when you shift your focus from what's gone to what's still possible. Acknowledge your feelings, but don't let that sorrow close you off to hope.

MYTHICAL MESSAGE Grief and loss are part of the journey, but they don't define it. There is still something to hold on to—look for it.

AFFIRMATION

even in sorrow, I find strength

six of cups
reflection

memory, innocence, emotional roots, comfort

Three mermaids float together in a loose circle, arms held high, surrounded by cups and scattered blossom. Above them, a dolphin leaps through the sunlight, breaking the surface of the water with ease. The moment feels trouble-free and familiar, like something from the past that still makes you smile when it comes back around.

MEANING Nostalgia is knocking and arrives with memories of the past. The Six of Cups invites reflection, but reminds you to stay balanced. There is always value in remembering, but life does go on. You could be reconnecting with old friends or revisiting childhood dreams—let these moments inspire your move forward, rather than trapping you in the past.

MYTHICAL MESSAGE Memories can be comforting, but they shouldn't keep you from the present. Take what's good from the past and bring it with you into the future.

AFFIRMATION

memories soften my heart, not my focus

seven of cups
vision

wishful thinking, dreaming, possibility, choices

A mermaid floats in the water, arms outstretched, as seven cups swirl around her. Inside each cup there is something different. She looks up, wide-eyed and unsure of whether to reach out or wait. The water holds them all for now, but not forever.

MEANING So many options, but which ones are real? The Seven of Cups represents dreams, possibilities, and illusions. This is exciting but can be overwhelming, so be mindful of wishful thinking. Take time to sort through your options carefully and choose wisely. Clarity and focus will turn your dreams into reality.

MYTHICAL MESSAGE Not everything is as it seems. If you're feeling unsure, take your time. The true opportunities will become clear when you trust yourself.

AFFIRMATION

I trust myself to see through illusion

eight of cups
change

letting go, moving on, detachment, spiritual quest

A lone merman rests at the water's edge, his focus on something in the distance. He is turned away from eight cups. A crescent moon hangs in the sky, casting a soft light over the water as he embraces a moment of stillness, a pause before moving on, following the pull of something deeper.

MEANING Change is coming and the time is right to move on. The Eight of Cups signals emotional growth and the courage you need to leave behind what no longer serves you. Although the journey ahead is pending, staying in the past will only hold you back. Trust yourself: Letting go creates space for something better.

MYTHICAL MESSAGE Walking away isn't failure; it's wisdom. If something no longer serves you, have the courage to leave it behind and seek what is truly fulfilling.

AFFIRMATION
I walk away from what no longer serves me

nine OF cups
thankfulness

pleasure, grace, emotional fulfillment, satisfaction

Beneath the sun's gentle glow, a mermaid floats with ease, framed by a gleaming arc of nine cups above her. There's serenity in her expression. She knows there is no need to reach for more at this point; she's taking in the beauty of what already is. Enjoying a moment of gratitude and grace.

MEANING Your wishes are within reach. The Nine of Cups brings satisfaction, gratitude, and emotional fulfillment. You are realizing that your goals or dreams have been achieved, so take time to appreciate what you've built. Stay humble, though, because true contentment comes from recognizing and valuing the abundance already in your life.

MYTHICAL MESSAGE This is your moment; pause and appreciate what you've created. Happiness isn't just about getting what you want; it's about recognizing what you have.

AFFIRMATION
I celebrate all I have created

ten of cups
alignment

happiness, safety, wholeness, family bonding

A family of merfolk gather at the water's surface, eyes lifted to the sky where a rainbow is beaming above and ten cups are nestled in its curve. Everything feels in sync: there's love, connection, and emotional ease. This is a moment of true alignment, in which each feels and shares their joy.

MEANING The Ten of Cups represents love, family, and the feeling of emotional security. Everything feels aligned and happiness flows effortlessly, filling your cup with emotional abundance from family, friends, or a partner. Embrace the joy that comes from unity, knowing that true happiness is found in shared moments and heartfelt bonds.

MYTHICAL MESSAGE Fulfillment lies in feeling at home within yourself and with those around you. Enjoy the love that surrounds you.

AFFIRMATION
love surrounds and sustains me

page OF cups
messenger

expression, positivity, surprise, creative spark

The Page floats under water, cradling a single cup in both hands. Fish and seahorses swirl around her playfully, drawn to her calm curiosity. There's wonder in her gaze, as if she's just heard something new. This is a moment of emotional openness, quiet magic, and fresh beginnings.

MEANING The Page of Cups invites you to embrace your imagination, explore your emotions, and stay open to new experiences. Positive news is coming: It could be a message of love, excitement, or emotional growth. Listen to your intuition and explore those fresh possibilities with creativity, curiosity, and an open heart.

MYTHICAL MESSAGE Life is offering you a moment of magic: an unexpected message, a creative idea, a chance to feel deeply. Pay attention.

AFFIRMATION
my inner child inspires fresh dreams

knight of cups
heartfelt

charm, romance, sensitivity, artistry

Beneath the waves, the Knight rides gracefully on the back of a seahorse, cup raised in one hand as if toasting a promise. He is moving through the shifting current with calm purpose, while being led by intuition and a big dream.

MEANING Intelligent but a dreamer, the Knight of Cups follows his heart. Be careful not to rush in and get swept off your feet! Embrace your emotions while taking care of your own feelings, and remember that actions always speak louder than words. Let inspiration guide you, but ensure your dreams have the foundation to become reality.

MYTHICAL MESSAGE Follow your heart, but don't get lost in dreams. Passion is powerful, but real progress comes when you move with both feeling and purpose.

AFFIRMATION
my passion guides me with grace

queen OF cups
intuitive

compassion, knowledge, empathy, kindness

The Queen sits on a rock raised from the ocean, while the sky turns stormy above. She holds a golden cup, eyes fixed on its depths, full of knowledge, inspiration, and spirituality. Her tail curls around her treasures. A delicate, crown-like headpiece rests in her hair; she rules not by force but through feeling.

MEANING Deeply intuitive and full of heart, the Queen of Cups reminds you to trust your emotions, taking care of yourself and those around you. She leads with empathy, offering wisdom through understanding. It's okay to let your feelings guide you, but don't forget to set healthy boundaries—balance is key. True strength isn't about being tough; it's about knowing yourself and staying open.

MYTHICAL MESSAGE Your intuition is speaking—listen. Emotional wisdom is your strength and your kindness has more impact than you realize.

AFFIRMATION

compassion is my superpower

king OF cups
understanding

support, balance, gentleness, wisdom

The King sits tall on a throne of coral, cup held gently in one hand while fish circle calmly around him. His focus is steady, not cold, and one full of deep knowing. He is still but not passive, secure in his wisdom and unmoved by the ebbs and flows of the water's current.

MEANING Calm, wise, and emotionally balanced, the King of Cups knows how to keep it together no matter what is going on around him. This card is a reminder to stay cool in tough situations, and that you can offer support without letting your emotions get the better of you. True leadership is about knowing when to step in with heart and when to think things through.

MYTHICAL MESSAGE Emotional strength comes from balance. Lead with wisdom, stay grounded in your feelings, and don't let emotions rule you—guide them instead.

AFFIRMATION
I lead with emotional balance and depth

ace OF wands
ideas

positivity, new beginnings, passion, new ventures

A phoenix hovers in flight, clutching a single glowing wand in its beak, focused as if it knows something important is about to begin. There is a feeling in the air as if a storm is coming. This is the moment before a bold idea takes flight.

MEANING A surge of energy and inspiration is here. The Ace of Wands signals new beginnings, fresh ideas, and a spark of creativity. This is your moment to trust your instincts to take action and follow your passion. The path ahead is full of potential—be open to opportunities and new friendships, because one idea or step forward could lead to something greater than you imagine. Embrace this moment with confidence and enthusiasm.

MYTHICAL MESSAGE A spark of inspiration is lighting the way. This is your sign to start. Go ahead and trust your passion. Take that first step.

AFFIRMATION

I'm inspired and ready to act

two OF wands
balance

inspiration, potential, planning, decisiveness

Floating quietly between two upright wands, wings held steady, the phoenix is not flying forward, but looking out, while carefully weighing things up. The energy is thoughtful and curious—you can almost feel the pause before movement begins.

MEANING You're standing at the edge of possibility, with the Two of Wands encouraging you to make bold decisions. You have options. Now's the time to choose your path and take the next step. Expand your vision and trust that the risks you take will set the foundation for long-term success. You have the ability to shape your future, so move forward with purpose.

MYTHICAL MESSAGE The world is opening up and the choice is yours. Step forward with confidence because your future is shaped by your vision.

AFFIRMATION
the world opens when I step forward

three OF wands
travel

processing, foresight, adventure, momentum

The phoenix is taking a moment to survey all that is on the horizon, considering the next adventure, with wings tucked in and looking relaxed as three wands surround it. There's nothing frantic here; just focus and poise.

MEANING Your plans are taking shape. The Three of Wands signals expansion and progress, allowing you to look ahead with confidence. Whether it's travel or a new venture, this card encourages patience, and trust in a journey that will broaden your horizons. Keep your vision clear and motivations high. The efforts you have made will soon bear fruit.

MYTHICAL MESSAGE Momentum is building and your plans are taking shape. Keep looking ahead because your next adventure is closer than you think.

AFFIRMATION
I trust the momentum I've built

four OF wands
movement

harmony, friendship, satisfaction, happiness

With wings spread and in full flight, the phoenix soars above open fields, the four wands just ahead to provide guidance and direction. The energy is calm and the scene feels like a homecoming, bringing the celebration of something well-earned.

MEANING The Four of Wands signals a time of harmony and celebration. It marks joy-filled milestones with parties, friendships, and a sense of belonging. Recharge and strengthen those connections that give you contentment. It's important to appreciate how far you've come and to celebrate your achievements, both personal and professional.

MYTHICAL MESSAGE There's joy in the air, so pause and celebrate. No matter how big or small, you should recognize the moments that make life feel truly good.

AFFIRMATION
joy lives in the moment

five OF wands
tension

conflict, disengagement, struggle, challenge

Mid-flight, the phoenix struggles to keep the five wands together and they are falling from its grasp. Its wings are flared and ready to challenge. This could be training or a real battle, but either way the scene is unsettling and full of conflicting energies.

MEANING There's a struggle for control, whether it's external conflict or inner tension. The Five of Wands signals a testing time full of competition and clashing ideas. You may feel at odds with others, or even yourself, being pulled in multiple directions. If you can separate yourself from unnecessary battles, you will find clarity. Focus on constructive solutions rather than getting lost in the chaos.

MYTHICAL MESSAGE Not every challenge is a battle. Step back, refocus, and ask yourself: Is this worth my energy, or is it just noise?

AFFIRMATION
I embrace challenge without chaos

six OF wands
progress

triumph, self-confidence, success, good news

The phoenix flies confidently and triumphantly, clutching one wand tightly in its claws. Below, the other wands flow freely, almost in recognition of the progress that has been made, being seen for showing up and doing the work.

MEANING It's game, set, and match with the Six of Wands, bringing success, recognition, and confidence in your achievements. Your hard work is paying off. You deserve it and now others are noticing. Trust in your progress, but stay humble—this is just one milestone on your journey. Keep moving forward with self-assurance.

MYTHICAL MESSAGE You've worked hard and now this shows. Stand tall in your success, but remember that true confidence comes from within and not just through recognition.

AFFIRMATION
success feels better when shared

seven OF wands
challenge

defense, obstacle, persistence, overwhelmed

Flying head on, the phoenix grips a wand for protection and holds its wings open in defiance. The other wands are pointing upward and pushing back. There's a challenge here, but the phoenix isn't retreating. Instead, it's standing its ground, even when outnumbered.

MEANING The fight isn't over yet. The Seven of Wands signals a challenge; perhaps you feel overwhelmed or under attack. Stand your ground and defend your position with confidence. You've come too far to back down now. With persistence and resilience, you will rise above the obstacles. Your determination will shape your success, so believe in yourself and keep moving.

MYTHICAL MESSAGE The pressure is on, but you're stronger than you know. Hold your ground, trust yourself, and don't let your doubts overwhelm you.

AFFIRMATION

holding my ground is part of the journey

eight OF wands
speed

travel, frustration, sudden change, excitement

Eight wands streak through the sky in one direction, fast and clear. The phoenix stands ready, watching. Everything's in motion now, and the phoenix knows this is not the moment to interrupt.

MEANING Things are suddenly moving very quickly in all areas of your life! The Eight of Wands represents rapid progress, messages, and momentum. Whether it's through travel or a change in direction, life is definitely picking up speed. However, you could experience some feelings of impatience and frustration. Trust the flow and ride the wave, staying focused and adaptable as events unfold.

MYTHICAL MESSAGE Things are moving quickly—stay focused, stay ready. There could be a new opportunity or challenge coming; this is your moment to act.

AFFIRMATION
I move with purpose and clarity

nine OF wands
brave

courage, test of faith, resilience, endurance

Laying wounded and resting, the phoenix's head is supported by one wand, while the other wands are arranged in a semicircle like a wall of protection. The air is heavy with tiredness, but the phoenix is not ready to give up yet.

MEANING You are battle-worn and have made some sacrifices, but you are not defeated. The Nine of Wands is a test of endurance, telling you that now is the time to summon your courage. You've overcome so much. Don't give up now, as you're closer than you think! Trust in your resilience and know that this challenge is shaping you into someone even stronger.

MYTHICAL MESSAGE You've come so far and it's important that you don't stop now! Yes, you're tired, but resilience is your greatest strength. One last push and you're there.

AFFIRMATION

resilience is my power

ten OF wands
release

complexity, weight of the world, delegation, burden

With all ten wands bundled in its claws, the phoenix presses on. Nothing's falling, but it's a lot to carry. The movement is slow and deliberate, with wings fully stretched—this journey is arduous but almost over.

MEANING The burden feels heavy and the pressure is piling up. The Ten of Wands warns against carrying too much alone. You are caught up in the minor details, so it's time to lighten the load. Look at the bigger picture and put yourself first. Prioritize, then release what no longer serves you. Freedom comes with letting go.

MYTHICAL MESSAGE The weight feels heavy. Ask yourself: Am I carrying too much? If so, let go of what isn't yours to hold.

AFFIRMATION
I release what I don't need to carry

page OF wands
free-spirited

impulsiveness, flexibility, energy, discovery

The Page stands with her wand in both hands, as if she's figuring out what to do next. The phoenix perched on top of the wand feels more like a friend than just a guide. There's curiosity in the Page's face: Not everything is certain, but she's ready to try.

MEANING Curious and adventurous, the Page of Wands is ready to explore new opportunities and keen to succeed. It's important that you embrace this free-spirited nature and the new experiences that await, but be mindful of impulsiveness. Remain flexible because life is full of surprises, and adaptability will be your greatest strength.

MYTHICAL MESSAGE Adventure is calling, so say yes to something new. Follow your curiosity and trust that you'll figure things out along the way.

AFFIRMATION
I follow with curiosity without overthinking

knight OF wands
present

adventurous, forthright, bold, rebellious

Riding fast on the back of a soaring phoenix, the Knight grips his wand, bold and brave. He's enjoying the wind in his face and fire at his feet, with no intention of slowing down. There's determination here, but also a bit of chaos.

MEANING Bold, passionate, and eager for adventure, the Knight of Wands is always on the move. This card is full of energy and action, and the Knight urges you to seize the moment and act with confidence as you work toward completing your goals. However, be mindful: Acting too fast without planning ahead can lead to setbacks. Enjoy the journey but stay aware of the bigger picture.

MYTHICAL MESSAGE Go boldly, but don't burn out. Passion will take you far, but make sure your actions match your long-term vision.

AFFIRMATION

I am ready for adventure

queen OF wands
in control

approachable, natural, thriving, charismatic

The Queen sits proudly on a throne of lava, wand resting easily in one hand. She doesn't need to do much to be noticed; there's a warmth and confidence in how she holds herself. She is in full control amid the heat.

MEANING A leader with warmth and strength, the Queen of Wands is confident, magnetic, and in command of her own life. She balances authority and approachability with a dedicated nature that is inspiring to others. This card wants you to step into your power, embracing your natural talents and trusting in your abilities. Confidence is magical—when you believe in yourself, or someone else, others will too.

MYTHICAL MESSAGE Confidence looks good on you. Trust your abilities and own your space, knowing that your warmth and presence inspire others.

AFFIRMATION
I radiate confidence and creativity

king of wands
wholesome

decisive, authoritative, visionary, entrepreneurial

Facing straight ahead, the King sits solidly on a throne of lava, wand held upright in his hand. There's no need to overexplain his presence, as it speaks for itself—he is relaxed, yet alert, and always ready to take action when needed.

MEANING A visionary and a natural leader, the King of Wands is decisive, bold, and inspiring. He sees the bigger picture and takes action with authority, looking for practical solutions to help solve problems and offering guidance. As a card of confidence and integrity to stand up for what you believe in, it's time to make decisions that shape your future, so approach them with purpose and wisdom.

MYTHICAL MESSAGE Lead with vision, not just action. People look up to you; set the tone, take charge, and build something truly meaningful.

AFFIRMATION
I lead with vision and courage

ace of pentacles
wealth

opportunity, riches, stability, new ventures

In a quiet clearing, two dryads carry a single glowing pentacle between them. They are holding the pentacle carefully, as if they know it's valuable. The energy is grounded and new, and full of potential.

MEANING A new door to prosperity and opportunity is opening. The Ace of Pentacles heralds financial growth, career opportunities, or a fresh start. It's a time of optimism and a chance to maximize your blessings. Wealth isn't just about money; it's also about security and long-term success. Nurture this opportunity with dedication and it will flourish into something abundant and long-lasting.

MYTHICAL MESSAGE A fresh opportunity is coming with promises of growth and stability. Whether financial or personal, take this seriously; it could be the foundation for something that endures.

AFFIRMATION
I plant seeds for lasting growth

two OF pentacles
juggling

adaptability, flow, flexibility, priorities

A beautiful tree nymph juggles two pentacles, which loop in the air, creating a soft infinity symbol. Her arms move with ease, but you can see the effort behind this. She's keeping things in flow, but it's a delicate balance. The motion is maintained—for now.

MEANING Life is a balancing act, and the Two of Pentacles needs you to stay flexible. Whether managing finances, work, or life's everyday responsibilities, adaptability is key. If you feel stretched too thinly, prioritize wisely and go with the flow. You will find balance through organization and a steady approach, especially when it comes to finances.

MYTHICAL MESSAGE Life is demanding, but you're managing it well. Stay flexible and trust yourself to handle the shifts. Balance comes from knowing what truly matters.

AFFIRMATION
I find my flow amid the juggling

three OF pentacles
triumph

collaboration, unity, contribution, synergy

Filled with laughter and celebration, three dryads play with pentacles alongside small forest creatures. The energy is creative and collaborative. The squirrel brings resourcefulness while the birds nod to freedom through creativity, each bringing something unique. This isn't quite work, and it's not quite play, but it feels as if the dryads are building something together.

MEANING Success comes through teamwork. The Three of Pentacles recognizes the joy that comes from collaboration, sharing skills, and building something greater together. This card wants you to value the input of others, whether that's at work or in your personal projects. By combining talents, you'll achieve more than you could alone.

MYTHICAL MESSAGE Great things happen when people come together. Learning from a mentor or working as a team will reveal that a shared effort brings the best results.

AFFIRMATION
collaboration raises us higher

four OF pentacles
investment

blocking growth, money, security, conservation

Standing tall and stable, while balanced on two pentacles, the dryad holds a third pentacle in his hands. There's a sense he could be holding on tightly, perhaps for safety or maybe from habit. Behind him, a larger pentacle glows, casting light through the forest and illuminating his focus. He's reflecting and not quite ready to make a move. In the distance, a stag watches over him, guarding his energy and bringing strength and balance to his life.

MEANING Have you been keeping your wallet firmly closed recently? The Four of Pentacles warns against financial or emotional rigidity. Saving and security are important, but clinging to what you have can block future growth. It might be time to think about where you can invest a little—whether that's your money, time, or energy—to create long-term abundance.

MYTHICAL MESSAGE Holding on too tightly? Money, control, or old habits can keep you stuck. Be mindful of what you're protecting and consider whether it's helping or holding you back.

AFFIRMATION
I protect what I've built but remain open

five OF pentacles
pride

financial loss, frugality, hardship, isolation

Two figures stand beneath a tree in an icy forest, shoulders slumped, faces full of hardship. The five pentacles sit high in the branches, visible but out of reach. Overhead, two crows watch quietly, messengers of transformation, insight, and unseen guidance. The figures are not without hope, but at the moment it's a struggle.

MEANING A period of hardship may have left you feeling isolated. The Five of Pentacles speaks of financial struggles or emotional scarcity. You could be worried about work and losing your job or about an important relationship, but support is available if you're willing to ask. Caution can help you rebuild, but don't let pride stop you seeking help when needed.

MYTHICAL MESSAGE It is okay to struggle, but it's also okay to ask for support. Help is closer than you think; reach out and find your way forward.

AFFIRMATION

I reach out when I need support

six OF pentacles
giving

generosity, sharing, fairness, humility

A hooded figure stands tall, his face hidden. He clutches three pentacles in his hands while three more hover behind him. Two dryads kneel before him, their hands open and reaching out, hoping and waiting for a share of his wealth.

MEANING The balance of giving and receiving is at play here. The Six of Pentacles points toward generosity, whether that's an offer of help or accepting it. Wealth, time, or knowledge shared wisely creates a beautiful cycle of abundance. If you have more than enough, give freely; if you're in need, be open to receiving.

MYTHICAL MESSAGE Life flows in cycles; sometimes you give, sometimes you receive. Whether offering support or accepting it, trust that generosity creates abundance for everyone.

AFFIRMATION

I give and receive with balance

seven of pentacles
future

profit, advantage, investment, patience

In a quiet moment, a lone dryad is taking in the fruits of his labor. The trees around him are heavy with pentacles; one has fallen to the ground and is resting in front of him. There is a feeling of both fatigue and satisfaction here. Near his feet a hedgehog watches on, a symbol of self-discovery and the determined pursuit of purpose.

MEANING Your efforts are beginning to bear results. The Seven of Pentacles is a sign to step back, assess your progress, and plan for the future. Success doesn't come overnight, but a glimpse of what's to come shows that patience and perseverance will bring long-term rewards. Keep investing in what's working and adjust where needed.

MYTHICAL MESSAGE Your efforts are paying off, even if you can't see the full picture yet. Take a moment to reflect; patience now will bring bigger rewards later.

AFFIRMATION
growth isn't always loud

eight OF pentacles
dedication

skills, apprenticeship, refinement, commitment

Sitting low to the ground, a dryad is painting a pentacle, while many more surround him. His focus is deep and he is unaware of the rabbits and squirrel watching on as he works, symbols of the manifestation of his toils and the excitement of what is to come. This is steady work that requires stillness. You get the sense he'll be here for a while, and that's okay.

MEANING Hard work and mastery go hand in hand. The Eight of Pentacles signals a period of learning; maybe you want to refine a skill or build on your expertise. Being dedicated and taking pride in your work will lead to the skillfulness you seek. Whether it's your craft, career, or personal growth, keep at it; your efforts will pay off.

MYTHICAL MESSAGE You're in a period of learning and growth. Keep refining your craft and trust that mastery comes with dedication, time, and effort.

AFFIRMATION
progress comes from dedication

nine of pentacles
gratitude

self-sufficiency, luxury, appreciation, abundance

Dancing freely, a tree nymph opens her arms to the forest around her. Pentacles follow one of her waving arms while a small phoenix perches lightly on her other hand. With flowers swirling all around her, she's in her element, at ease, unbothered, and grounded in her own beautiful space.

MEANING You're so close to where you want to be, and it's time to appreciate those achievements. The Nine of Pentacles is all about gratitude, independence, and enjoying the fruits of your hard work. You've put in the effort, and now you get to enjoy the rewards. Take a moment to feel proud of what you've built and treat yourself; it's okay to enjoy and be thankful after the struggles along the way.

MYTHICAL MESSAGE You've worked hard to create this life, so enjoy it. Independence and comfort aren't just about wealth, but also about appreciating what you've built for yourself.

AFFIRMATION

I enjoy the results of my work

ten of pentacles
legacy

family unit, inheritance, completion, flow

Beneath an arch of pentacles, a family of dryads stands together. In front of them, a peaceful landscape full of fields and mountains stretches farther than the eye can see—it is their home, their legacy for their descendants. The energy is warm, complete, and shared. This is where things settle.

MEANING Security and family wealth come into focus here. The Ten of Pentacles represents long-term success, stability, and the rewards of past efforts coming to completion. There may be a retirement, or work on a family legacy or inheritance, but this card reminds you to appreciate the foundation you've built and to invest in what truly lasts: family, community, and security.

MYTHICAL MESSAGE Success is more than personal gain; it's also about lasting security and the people who matter. Look at what you've built and the legacy you want to leave behind.

AFFIRMATION
I invest in what lasts

page of pentacles
proposals

*establishment, new doorways, ambition,
intellectual growth*

In a snow-covered forest, a glowing pentacle hovers just above the Page's open hands, as if she's just received it or is about to pass it on. Her gaze is steady. She's not in a rush; it's as if she's just getting started and understands how much the next step matters.
At her feet, mice are reminding the Page to notice the small details in life that often go unseen, while a fox peeks from behind a tree, carrying the quiet wisdom of change and adaptability.

MEANING A new opportunity is taking shape: Is it good news or a wish fulfilled? The Page of Pentacles signals the beginning of something promising; it could be a career move, a fruitful financial venture, or the realization of a personal goal. There are still some things to work through, but stay focused and eager to learn. The doors opening now will lead to long-term stability if you're willing to put in the hard work.

MYTHICAL MESSAGE New possibilities are taking shape, but you need to put in the effort to help them grow. Be open to learning and take that first step forward.

AFFIRMATION
every small step is progress

knight OF pentacles
methodical

productive, steady, practical, focused

The Knight sits with a sure posture atop a winged horse, holding a pentacle high in the air. The ground below is stable. There's no rush, more a steady forward motion and attention to detail. This isn't about speed; it's about reaching the destination with focus.

MEANING Slow and steady wins the race. The Knight of Pentacles is diligent, hardworking, and committed to the long game. You're on the right track and success doesn't come from shortcuts but from consistent effort. There is a good opportunity on the horizon, so keep moving forward methodically because your discipline will lead to lasting rewards.

MYTHICAL MESSAGE Progress comes from consistent effort. Keep going, trust yourself, and know that success builds over time.

AFFIRMATION
I move steadily, building something solid

queen OF pentacles
contentment

down-to-earth, caring, nurturing, self-worth

Seated on a wooden throne, the Queen turns gently to one side, holding a pentacle in her lap. She looks calm but capable: She is a presence that makes everything around her feel settled. There's warmth in her space. She is grounded, present, and knows what she's tending to.

MEANING Warm, practical, and full of wisdom, the Queen of Pentacles is the heart of a home and the rock of a community. She encourages you to take care of yourself and others, and to create a life that brings contentment, fulfillment, and security. Success isn't always about money, and this card is a reminder to stay grounded and nurture the people who make your life rich and meaningful.

MYTHICAL MESSAGE You have a natural gift for creating comfort and security, with a steadiness that is a source of strength for others.

AFFIRMATION

my caring creates comfort and success

king OF pentacles
recognition

reliability, fatherliness, leadership, stability

Facing forward from a wooden throne, the King sits with relaxed authority, a pentacle hovering between his hands. Surrounded by lush foliage, his gaze is direct, but also kind and rooted. This is someone who built what he has, and holds it with care.

MEANING A symbol of stability and success, the King of Pentacles brings reliability, wisdom, and a strong foundation. He may appear as a fatherly figure or mentor, guiding you toward long-term growth. This card is about steady leadership, with patience and the ability to make smart decisions that will stand the test of time. Trust in your abilities and be confident that you can handle whatever life sends your way.

MYTHICAL MESSAGE You've built something solid through wisdom and hard work. Lead with confidence and enjoy the stability you've created.

AFFIRMATION

I lead with grounded confidence

acknowledgments

I'd like to thank my publisher—Carmel, Imogen, and the whole team at CICO Books for helping to bring my vision to life. Huge thanks to my agent, Chelsey Fox, for her support throughout.

Special thanks to Julia for her incredible illustrations, and to Josie for her help with content and inspiration. I'm also grateful to my wonderful team of readers and the ever-supportive office staff.

And lastly, to my fiancé, Lee—thank you for everything.

ABOUT THE ILLUSTRATOR

Julia Cellini is a watercolorist and illustrator whose work is inspired by the natural world and the local flora and fauna where she lives in Hawaii, USA.